Love
Loss

Luise Thomas

Camrose Press

Copyright © Luise Thomas 2018
ISBN: 978-1-9996002-0-4
First Published 2018
Camrose Press, Camrose Farm,
Camrose, Haverfordwest,
Pembrokeshire SA62 6JA
camrosepress@gmail.com
www.facebook.com/luisemargaret/
www.luisethomas53.wordpress.com

LEGAL NOTICE
All rights reserved. No part of this book may be reproduced, stored in a retrieval system, or transmitted in any form or by any means, electronic, mechanical, photocopying, recording or otherwise, without prior written permission from Camrose Press.

Luise Thomas has asserted her right under Section 77 of the Copyright, Designs and Patents Act 1988 to be identified as the author of this work.

Printed by Forrest Print, Milford Haven, Pembrokeshire.

Foreword

...the (poet's) voice is unlike any other voice you have ever heard and it is speaking directly to you, communing with you in private, right in your ear...

Al Alvarez, *The Writer's Voice*,
(Bloomsbury, 2006,p.15)

I want to be that voice in your ear.

To Larry, Irene, Helen & Alex, with my love Lo xxxx

for Amelia and Tony
for my family and friends
for me
for you

Contents

The Path Not Followed	1
Hand-made	2
The Tree of Life	4
Measurements	5
How	6
Fox Trail	7
The Old Man	8
African	10
Eighteenth Birthday	12
How to fly	13
Friend	14
Man	15
The Here and Now	16
Death in Spring	17
Breakfast	18
Doorway	19
Friends Re-united	20
B.S.T.	21
Severn Bridge	22
Lady Moon	23
Today and Tomorrow	24
Requiem	25
Pat in Spring/Generation Gap	26
Mother's Comfort	27
Leycesteria	28
Swimming	29
Centenary WW1	30
Birchbark	31
The Tree of Love	32
Visiting the Celtic Cross on Islay	33
Proposal Pending	34
Bedmaking	35
Andrew Wyeth's Woman	36
New Friends	37
My Unknown Grandmother	38
Gaps	39
Mousehole Moon and Sun	41

Excommunication	42
Throwback	43
Conkers	44
Starlings	45
Mexican Wedding	46
May contain imperfections. Wash before use.	47
Chaos in Camrose	48
Winter	50
Twelfth Night	51
Transmogrification	52
Brother-at-war	53
Mother Nature	54
The Tree of Loss	55
Take me with you	56
About the Author	57
Thanks	58

The Path Not Followed

I have set out too late
to take the long avoided
signposted path
the well- trodden way
the scenic route
the one with the guides
who tell you when to stop
take in the views
those they consider essential
I have no time to clamber
over their carefully constructed styles
pass through their gateways
permitting access
to continue
gratified
by their patronage

I must take the short cut
strike out
across country
find my own path
struggle
with unfamiliar terrain
scramble over ditches
through hedges
over fences
trust my own compass
to lead me
on.

Hand-made

The well-crafted pieces-
textiles, garments,
approved by Morris's tenets-
beautiful, useful,
-these are good.

Our home,
self- built of wood,
block and plaster,
- borne of our love
filled with our laughter-
dancing in the kitchen,
singing on the stairs,
-this is better.

My garden,
carved from the field,
roses sprung from cuttings,
ferns from friends,
seeds sown,
soul grown
-this is necessary.

The ultimate wonder-
my miracle child,
conceived against the odds,
nurtured to womanhood,
creative and caring,
-she is amazing.

But this,
these insistent lines
that show who I am,
that drag me from sleep,
demand to be channelled,
this well of words,
that rise through my dreams,
flow through my arm,

to my hand,
to the page,
to be sung by my voice,
or gift wrapped
for others
and read by their choice
-this is a mystery.

The Tree of Life

The trees of my childhood were not for climbing,
the grass for keeping off.
One limb we swung down from-
over the playground wall to the bus stop below.
When we moved to the country
climbing seemed overrated,
no thrill in it.
Hedgerow trees were small
compared to London planes
and unforbidden.
A few years more,
trees were for lying under
heavily petting
under the cover of clothing.
Protected, from the prying eyes
of passing walkers,
by the broad oak.
Much later
came the realisation
that I am drawn to trees,
as I am drawn to the sea,
to the earth.

Measurements

At ten I swam the width
across a Dorset bay
my 'uncle', six months
married to my mum
swam beside me
his breath as loud as whale-blow
my dad six years absent
it was a serious endeavour
a mile at least
a gull screeched its warning
as we scrunched Jurassic pebbles
down to the chilly tide
Mum was stationed at the other side
with towels, soup, sandwiches
my younger brother
ballooning her belly
the older pair
fishing from the rocks
I grew two more decades
before I knew my true paternity
half another
and I had lost him
two Dads down.

How

How many moments
would sum the total
of our knowingness
how many hours, days, weeks,
years?

How many walks
have we not taken
but lain in a particular field
under a particular tree
watched by those particular cattle?

How many dependencies
did you awaken in me?
How many memories held by these fingers,
the hollow of your chest
your thigh, your smile?

How deeply did you etch
the pattern of my life
on my then
unblemished soul?

Fox Trail

I followed in the vixen's path
and wondered would she heed my scent
when she next delicately
picked her way across our field
would she give thought to what heavy creature
had blundered through her meandering territory
which sways with yorkshire fog and crested dog tail
-as meadows should.
Would the rattle seeds which filled my shoes
stick between her hardened pads?
And come the day, which soon it will,
will she stare bemused at the shorn sward,
the altered landscape bereft of sanctuary?
Soon I will wait patiently
while my busy man fills the trailer
then drive two tractor lengths behind -
content to play the farmer's wife,
happy with my part in the harvest.

The Old Man

We called him the old man
but he never got to be one
left his party early
younger than I am now
the first I knew
he was ill
was an unfinished meal
he'd appeared on my doorstep
hundreds of miles from his own
thought he'd pop in
he was halfway anyway
slept for an hour
then drove back
leaving his afterimage
in the doorway
it gave me time
that inkling
to talk about avoided things
paternity and lies
grasp a new memory
a jumble sale
a walk
the gift of his village
he didn't make a fuss
he knew there could be worse
horrific accidents
hideous guilt
a bit of pain
could be endured
"what's a bit of pain
compared to the man up the road
killed his child
reversing out of his drive-
how do you live with that?"
I wasn't told he was dying
'til I phoned on fathers' day
I raced to his deathbed
sang him to sleep

soon it will be three decades
he's been in my thoughts
visited my dreams
like that time on my doorstep
briefly present
then slipped away
with no resolution
to my unanswered questions
why lie when the truth is good enough?

African

My hips have swayed
to African music,
my soul responds
to African drums.

I wept at the plight
of Nelson Mandela
and the African children
shot as they run.

I chose to refuse
South African produce
when South Africans
had no choice to be free.

I taught the children
African dances,
I sing my own
an African song.

I cried with joy
when the African people
chose to be led
by their African son.

And when I read
the African woman,
I know part of her
and I, are one.

So why,
- when the African comes to my doorway-
does the history of Empire
re-visit me
and my parents' prejudice
make his African skin
the first thing
 I see?

I buy,
he smiles,
happily leaving me
with my shame.

Eighteenth Birthday

Being your Mum
is the best thing
that I have ever done.
For you are
a beautiful,
clever,
shining star.
So, whatever you do
-as your utterly gorgeous self-
and wherever you go,
I will see you shine
and I will know
that you are also
my unique treasure,
precious child of mine.

How to Fly

First break into a slow run,
skip a bit then jump
higher, to a vertical take off
(your heart will lurch a bit).
Then swim in the air
-pulling a strong breaststroke
to gain height.

When you're up,
gaze down
at the familiar streets below.
Be invisible.
Follow your usual routes
so as not to lose yourself.
Keep a steady pace,
let giggling bubbles
fill your hollow bones.

Return to where you started,
tread air as you descend.
Feel happy, secretive, graceful.
Walk on smiling.
Try not to wake.

Friend

my friend is a tree standing tall and strong that I can lean and rest upon until the strong winds blow and shake the branches ripping through the sturdy boughs so that the strengths I thought I'd found are torn like fragile leaves that flutter helpless to the ground

Man

And is there a man in your life?
Well dozens I said
all mostly in my past

some like my father, dead
though he still visits my present
drops comfortably into my dreams
giving bizarre advice
and a cheery wave

a few in my present
my brothers, some excellent friends
a current disappointment
who it has to be said
still hands the occasional morsel
to keep my hopes fed

and one in the future?
Possibly maybe
the longed-for comforter
sympathiser jester
playmate friend
the one to bring the weary trail to its end
is there a prize
a reward for my strife
is there indeed a man for my life?

The Here and Now

I'm here now
and I found him
he is my treasure
and I am his
so, I can forgive you
I don't hurt anymore
I hardly think of you
and never with anger
nor regret
you were simply
a stone in the path
stumbled over
then resolutely left behind
all of you.

Death in Spring

It goes against nature to be dying in spring-
to be fading while all around is burgeoning.
The earth gradually dons her wedding attire-
pale pinks, bright yellows, soft greens,
the occasional splash of red-
while we finger our sad dark suits with dread-
against the time when we will gather,
ashamed to be glad to be together,
the present survivors still here to mourn.
We, who wait in this current limbo
while nature
goes about her business.
The sap continues its urgent rise,
while we hold our collective breaths
for news of your demise.

Breakfast

My mum came home today -
a brief visit
from that hazy horizon
she lives on.
We talked as we used to talk,
cosy amongst the breakfast debris,
the kettle puttering on the Aga.

She, in her dressing gown,
me, in gardening garb.
She, lucid and engaged,
me, stunned and amazed.

In those precious moments
she gave me permission
to be free.
And I wept,
in the sudden knowledge
of how much
I miss her.

Doorway

She is not gone yet
our love can't lead her back through
our perceived portals.

Friends Re-united

Old friends
(now older friends)
like
re-discovered favourite garments
hung for a few seasons
at the back of the wardrobe
mournfully thought out-grown
now joyously slipped back on
and found an even better fit
more assuredly worn
confident that the weight and drape
hang perfectly from the shoulder
hem swirling as we turn to stride on.

B.S.T.

Today it is Spring!
I can't bear to be in,
I need to be out
bathing in bright, bright light
warm enough to flout
the old wives,
cast two clouts-
despite the bite
in the breeze
and the thorny may
that chides us
don't be fooled.
A bee has bumbled
onto the green sheet
as I peg,
the cats cavort-
in and out
of unaccustomed open doors-
chattering at joyful birdsong
bemused by the timing out of whack.
Today it is Spring
tomorrow, Winter may be back.

Severn Bridge

As a child she watched that bridge grow
between the here and there.
Crossing on the oily ferry,
not knowing then that there, would become here.
Loving the here fiercely now,
possessively, as adopters do-
claiming it as her own, despite the disparate voice
which she ceased to know she possessed,
taken by surprise when confronted
by its affronted fifth- generation, true possessors.
She crossed that bridge back and fore,
here, becoming there, as a second bridge grew,
merging there into here, until the chasm healed
and she knew where she belonged.

Now she finds herself on another bridge.
Two other women traverse with her
yet travelling in opposite directions.
The one born here, the other there,
a woman-child and a child-woman.
She remains in the center,
becoming the cables, suspending the bridge-
yet more organic than drawn steel.
Her cables are vine, ivy, sinews, heartstrings.
Supporting them both on their journey-
the child -woman toward independence and her life,
the woman-child to dependence and after.
She is both bridge and suspended traveler,
supporting them both, torn by both.
Her own life interrupted as she tautens and sags,
fearful of the end of one and the beginning of the other
yet desiring the continuation of her own journey across the bridge.
Not heeding the occasional urge to jump off.

Lady Moon

The moon tonight
is wearing her slightly worried face-
almost full.
I am relinquished from
your long- ago admonition,
that old wives' tale,
not to look at the new moon through glass
for risk of calamity.
How could I not,
bespectacled as I am and was?

We thought we would always be friends
yet we drifted apart.
I thought you so wise,
you thought me so …what?
Our mutual admiration
soon eclipsed.

I talk to you through the cosmos,
light years pass by your reply
yet the same moon
still
hangs above us both.

Today and Tomorrow

Today I walk
in the spaces
my first child
will walk in
tomorrow
a slip in time
my shadow
will linger
for her
to slip into
we remain
disconnectedly
connected
not my child
but ever my daughter.

Requiem

Handsome man, sexy dancer,
lip kisser, big hugger.
I never heard him raise his voice.
He'd greet my dramas- joy or woe-
with his sanguine smile,
listen well, think awhile,
give his counsel with a nod of the head,
knew that soonest mended
always meant least said.

Calm, slow, sure, unruffled,
for years he gently stepped aside,
let death pass.
I'm fine, you go ahead
I'm not quite ready yet.

He holds my gaze
from our wedding photo throng
and in this precious moment
he is not gone.

Pat in Spring/ Generation Gap

I won't want to be poetic when you've gone
my heart will be prostrate with sorrow.
Now is the time to tell you-
(after you've modelled your elegant dress for flying off to Canada;
after you've told me your age is irrelevant;
after we've laughed and debated, hugged and shared;
after we've tussled with your title-
auntie, big sister, spare mum?
I've settled with darling friend.).
-that the love between us is broader than a poem can contain.

Mother's Comfort

I am not gone, darling daughter
I live on in you

 and in your darling daughter
 too

your brothers carry on their share
their children recite irreverent rhymes

throw back their heads
laugh like drains

before long you will think of me
and not be moved to weep

I won't command your thoughts
before and after sleep

you'll smile at the red and orange last light
reflected on wet sand

a yellow rose will be
just a yellow rose in your hand

my photos will shine
 you will too

remember my failings with a wry smile
know that I loved you

your grief will still ambush you
but wound you less

there will be laughter
I am in it.

Leycesteria

They say a pheasant's berry
can prove your friendship's true,
so, I've plucked a pheasant berry
and I'm sending it to you.
I've been working in my garden,
thinking of you all the while,
and the thoughts that I've been thinking
made me sit awhile and smile
about the things that we've got up to
in our present and our past
but I've sat and thought too long now
and I've got a grassy arse.
Now a 'gracias' is pleasant, when it's saying "I thank you"
but a "grass my arse" is funny
when your friend's got in a stew
about horticultural ignorance,
not knowing what is what
when it's growing in your shrubbery or growing in a pot.
Now, you're really very clever
when it comes to all that stuff
and it's evidently obvious that I don't know enough!
So, I take my hat off to you-
and I hope it makes you laugh-
hylocereus undatus var. 'Madam Grass My Arse'.

Swimming

I did not like gin
its taste too perfumed on my tongue
the tonic was ok
until the day
my brothers decreed
that gin must be
our mum's memorial toast
I complied
-what else?
it had changed
or else I had
and now
most nights
I swim in its depths
diving for pearls
with the taste
of my mother's scent.

Centenary WW1

It is right to celebrate
the end of that war,
good to honour the dead
but when we bow our heads
let it also be with shame
that war still happens
again, and again.
Once, just once in my life
-or did I dream it
(Christmas eve, '85?)
-the news announced,
No War Tonight!
No Armed Conflict in all the World!
A distant echo
of soldiers laying down arms to play,
refusing to fight on Christmas day.
If only that germ of sanity
could infect the earth-
a benign virus, a peace pandemic,
inoculating humanity against hate.

Birchbark

Do you remember
precious friend,
that time above the Sage,
beside the Tyne?
You, gathering birch bark,
declared it a page
worthy of poetry-
a thought I squirreled away
until today-
as, landscaping sorrow,
my silver darlings offered up this sheet,
it's bronzing pink face
sized to write.
My thoughts turned to you,
as they so often do
here in my garden.
I will not write of grief,
nor rage against the cruel thief
who stole her memory away.
But rather shout for light,
love, friendship, gardens!

The Tree of Love

We sat under a huge chestnut
wondering if we had time
to grow our own
to lean against
I bought one secretly
had it planted
on our first anniversary
while you were in the field
ten years old
to steal the march
on the time we lost before we met
you were confused and guilty
new to this marriage lark
not knowing that our wedding day
was something we should mark
you thought that building our house
was testament enough of your love
it was
it is
we are
our chestnut is big now
enough to sit under
lie under
love under.

Visiting the Celtic Cross on Islay

I whooped
at being a child again!
Sliding down the steep slope
under the enormous sky
above the naked bay
muddying my elderly bum
because my feet and legs
couldn't carry me
down and up
as they had
in our irreverent youth
plundering one monument
to make another
it's in the guide book now
so, we posed,
those of us that are left
grinning with our secret

forty years on
we are less and more
serious than then
more in tune with the elements
still politicking
still arguing
vying for attention
one-man upmanshipping
out performing
upstaging
saying we'll leave it to our kids
but not wanting to let go.

Proposal Pending

I went to a poetry festival
and bought a dress
but it's a poem of a dress
pale blue silk
embroidered on one side
fit for a mother
of a bride
I must hide it away
not let it be a jinx
while I prepare
to be a spare
to hand her
into the care
of her chosen
to become
her less significant mother

'til then we'll pin
our interests
drop hints
eat cake
go on a mother and daughter break
while we await
his bended knee.

Bedmaking

He stores things, my man.
Carefully dismantling
putting them aside for future consideration.
He made our bed
from the store-loft boards,
long hours of sanding,
smoothing the upper side
-ravaged by the wear and tear
of clogs and boots
weighted with sacks of corn-
refined them lovingly.
Traced the rough- hewn underside,
sensing the hands that had gone before,
acknowledging their investment
now in his custody.
Four long mortice joints
carved from the chocolate teak-
the wood so fine
it was more like sculpture than carpentry-
formed them to protect our dreams,
a solid frame to anchor us
through the uncharted hours
as we sail through sleep
as they once sailed.
Simple honest lines
against our whitewashed wall.
Seafaring decks
still seep their history
and cradle our dreams
to bring us safe to shore.

Andrew Wyeth's Woman

You've searched for me I know
years and years
since you first saw me
a double page spread
in that art student's room
you propped me up
while you were cleaning
asked him if you could borrow me
until your next visit
he shrugged
seemingly unsurprised
that a cleaner should be interested
in art
I've eluded you
even now
when images
are so easily come by
press a small button
type a few words
turn the key
up they come in front of your eyes
some you'd rather not see
but never me
never quite the woman you remember
who gazed back from the page
challenging you with her heartsore knowledge
think you've experienced life?
You know more now
closer to my age
than thirty- four years ago
I can't get any older
than when he pinned me to canvas
not so for you
each glance in the mirror
ages you.

New Friends

It's not easy
to make new friends
in later life
there's no shared history
no reminiscing
with luck
there's instant connection
glimpses of what's made us
and there's risk

I took one such
loved her quickly
-we'd barely declared
our friendship
when it got complicated

long car journeys
news to be digested
vigils to be kept
brine to be wept

but what is life
without loss

hiding from its riches
to stay safe

take the risk
be enriched.

My Unknown Grandmother

At fifteen, she moved
and the photograph was ruined
she moved
and the image was made
for me, proof
that she breathed
no lifeless tableau
of any May Queen and her maids
but her, fidgety,
the only one who disobeyed
the cloaked figure
behind the three-legged box

Now here, at twenty-five
smiling from ear to ear
extravagant headdress
huge bouquet
more maids
her dapper man
happiness her only plan

Now here at thirty-one
between the wars
a family portrait
my dad
with grubby socks
leaning into her
starry skirt

Now here at thirty-seven
more black on white
love's last gift
remembrance.

Gaps

In the spaces you no longer inhabit
I miss you most.
In the things I no longer do for you.

Light now dapples the stone wall
where once your pet's hutch stood.
Feeding him was a communion,
a daily link between us.

Perversely, I miss
the minor irritations
not there to rail against-
half- drunk tea
left to moulder.

My sad redundancy-
a selfish sense of loss-
is balanced by your joy,
your abundant happiness
at finding your place
beside your love.

There's still evidence
of your being here.
There will be many sorties yet
for things you need or want.
Much ferrying of stuff
from your ransacked room,
more hairgrips shed.

Before I reconfigure,
reorganise,
redistribute,
-to make the gaps
less gaping.

My constant companion
remains,

my shadow self,
the woman
I wish I had been,
reminding me
that I should have done
better
more.

The me who achieved her potential
and yours,
thwarted all the bullies,
protected us both
from hurt
-and worse.

The better woman
I wish I'd been,
mistress of her journey,
who stuck to a route.
Not misdirected,
storm tossed,
shipwrecked,
washed ashore.

I wish I had
arrived purposefully
at this safe- haven,
plotted my course,
steered us steadfastly.

Mousehole Moon and Sun

We arrived with the autumn equinox
moonful delight over the sea taking centre stage
spotlighting empty patches
nocturnal fishing boats missing their cue.

Waking with awe
at the fisherman's warning sky
we west coast dwellers,
accustomed to the hesitant
curtain call of the sun at end of day
-will he won't he,
slowly descending,
disappointing his audience,
slipping behind a cloud before his exit,
just a rosy afterglow giving faint applause-
see here, a bold crimson slash
announcing his entrance
he blinds us
as he climbs
spectacular
from his salty bath
in a swift ascent
to start the day.

Excommunication

I have been disconnected
something to do with the wiring
his not mine
it's unlikely
that normal service will be resumed
anytime soon

he's not talking
not explaining his ire
not to me
nor our brothers
it's his pain
a one- sided war
with me the only casualty

I'm keeping a tenuous connection
with the next generation
hoping that the links remain flexible enough
to be sustained
despite interference
from static friction.

Throwback

I read a footnote
on Richard Jeffries
and am thrown back to you
the first cut is the deepest

my long-matured recognition
of your teenaged pretension
mingles with the memory
of how you licked your lips
before we kissed
the tang of Gauloise
the way you walked
like a land-locked sailor
the cupping of my face
with your large hand
the lifting of my heart
at the sight of you

you abandoned me
the best love of my life will not
memories of you
feel like infidelity.

Conkers

You never know
when will be
the last cut
in October
days become shorter
the rain will fall
the lawn become
a shaggy rug
time in the garden
grows precious
I am grateful
for the chilly sun
the drying breeze
riding my mowing steed
avoiding the glowing conkers
dismounting to harvest their shine

I always hated Autumn
wanted to see it gone
hurry on through
winter so that
spring can come
now I've learned
to love it
knowing I'm in mine
each day, each hour
is precious
when you're running short of time.

Starlings

If I get my timing right
   I can stand in the lane
                and see them coming
   a murmurous dark cloud
      surging across the pale
     evening sky above me
        louder discernible notes now
     so close I could raise my hand
for them to flow around it like water
  then smoothing out to a ribbon
avian calligraphy in the sky
   curves and arcs and scrolls
  that flow around the Croft trees
to hug their silhouettes momentarily
     before dropping like fallen chiffon
which shatters to leaf the bare branches
   where an unseen hand
  abruptly switches off their clamour

                silence

       before the same hand claps
 to throw them back to the air as one
 shouting 'this is not the place!
this is not the place!'
 and the stream flows on.

Mexican Wedding

 Friends and family
gathered under a relentless sky
to hear the vows of a truculent boy
transformed
by the love of his
   glowing girl
                      the magnificent cardboard cake
                  stood witness to celebration
                      and mariachi
                      and feasting
                      and fizzing
                      and heat
                      and happiness
                      and dancing
the dancing!
What exuberant prancing!
        what thinly veiled sensuous expression of joy!
           Oh, how these Mexicans love to dance!
No waiting
to be swayed by alcohol -like our British boys
                    just play one note
and they're on the floor
                 not even the dance floor
                            just where
they stand
                  they give their partners their
hand
          and hips gyrate-
no effort required
     minimal footwork
               elegant hands
                   droop from flexible wrists
             their bodies are one
      sex on legs
          tantric salsa
             a dance of love

all night long.

May contain imperfections. Wash before use.

I'm sewing a scrap of sari
recycled
bought at a fair
I think it's silk
rolling a hem
between finger and thumb
neatening the three hacked edges
the fourth is faced with plain
to contrast the stylised iris
woven not printed
still bearing the dust
it was dragged in
Bangladesh-Birmingham
two spots of blood
a scratched gnat bite on your thigh
I stitch with embroidery thread
unknowingly bequeathed
I'll wear it at my wrinkling neck
a magenta bandage
bearing your blood
and the ghost of her fingers.

Chaos in Camrose

Hordes of men
have descended
big expensive
safety strapped
long lensed cameras
cradled in their hands
menacing tripods
across their shoulders
mayhem in our little village
cars abandoned
in our narrow lanes
who have they come
to persecute?
Who is the accused?
What murder done,
scandal exposed?

It's just a bird,
a small bird
with a funny face.
For this they have raced
across the country,
slept in their cars
under frozen stars,
to capture with their lenses,
note down in their books,
this little masked intruder
blown off course
to our sleepy rooves,
catching insects
in the cacophony
of clicking shutters.

Stay away from our gutters little bird!
Don't come near,
don't let our cats
become the villains of the piece!

On the 30th November 2016, the first masked wagtail known to have visited the U.K, (from its home in Kazakhstan), was spotted in our village.

Winter

I looked up
from my book
because a light
had switched on
I knew there was no light

it was the sun
suddenly released
from the cloud
opening his grey lid
making contact
eye to eye
through un-leaved
winter branches
low in the sky

I gazed steadfastly
uncaring that you shouldn't
look at him directly
two layers of glass
protected me

then a dimmer switch engaged
the light softened
faded
leaving tree silhouettes
consolation of winter
against the twilight sky.

Twelfth Night

It's time to take down Christmas
although it grieves my heart
I use my grandson's birthday
as a reason not to start
I should have been a Hindu
or Jewish-for the light
Hanukkah and Diwali
both make the winter bright
old Christmas must be put away
go forward with the year
I'll leave up one more string of lights
to make the nights less drear.

Transmogrification

I've lost it
but it's somewhere safe
it's bound to turn up soon
maybe it's behind the clock
up in Annie's room
I've rearranged the furniture
(without the aid of a saw)
I had to have a change
I couldn't stand it anymore
I've hidden all the ironing
where it's easy to ignore
'til it erupts over the the sofa
and we all will know the score.

I've donned my starry jumper
but with backward constellations
I've longed for the comfort of a fag
in stressful situations
I've confused my lovely grandson
with my not so lovely brother
that's it, I'm done, it's over,
I've turned into my mother.

Brother-at-war

I dream
of my brother
occasionally
I think
about him
constantly
he has imposed
this
premature grieving
I should feel
anger
but his
poisonous error
jealous rage
at imagined plots
outstrips us both
I am a child again
shut out
from his games
his club
his love

your love
your games
your club
you've shut me out
made me a child again
outstripped my sadness
with your anger
at imagined plots
your poisonous error
jealous rage
imposes
my
premature grief
constant thinking
occasional dreams
of you
my brother.

Mother Nature

She's slamming about again!
-thrown the chimney from our roof
rocked the willow from its roots
leaves are tumbling helpless
through the terrible sky
the chestnut's hula hooping
birds struggling to fly
she's unbolted the cap off the silo
the top could follow soon
she's dealing ridge tiles like a croupier
howling at the moon
she's flooding all the lowlands
showing us who's boss
one day we might realise
what's making her so cross.

The Tree of Loss

Plant me under the dancing ash
its keys will float and cover me
the sun will paint a dappled splash
plant me under the dancing ash
and I will lie quite still at last
underneath my final tree
plant me under the dancing ash
its keys will float and cover me.

Take me with you

Don't leave me behind

take me with you
up the hill
to breathe in the view
or stride along
the wind hurling beach
 taking the pulse of the tide

stand with glass
in hand
in the garden's last patch
of sun
by the wall
of old stone

dance me
around the kitchen
to the beat
of boiling
spuds

tell me
silly jokes
 hear my laugh

curl up with me
and the cats
purring in and out

say my name
keep me in mind.

About the author

Luise Thomas's C.V., from the age of thirteen, reads:
babysitter;
vet's receptionist;
French tutor;
mother's help;
record shop assistant;
bulb-picker;
au- pair;
office-worker;
telephonist/receptionist;
publisher's production manager;
advertising executive;
traveller;
folk-singer;
bar tender;
pub singer;
cleaner;
travelling hand-warmer-sales-person;
lawyer's receptionist;
recruitment executive;
weaver;
mother;
handywoman;
gardener;
qualified teacher;
carer;
farmer's wife.

Since the age of seven, she has also been a poet.

She lives in bliss with her husband, four cats and a Shire horse named Violet, on their farm in Pembrokeshire. Her beautiful daughter lives nearby, alongside her lovely chap. Her other beautiful daughter, her lovely chap, and two gorgeous grandchildren live near Manchester.

Luise is happy to engage in conversations about the poems and life experiences via camrosepress@gmail.com

Thanks

Thanks are due to my friends and family for their encouragement and support throughout this endeavour.
I thank them also for frequently being the inspiration behind the poems.
I am indebted to Samantha Wynne-Rhydderch, my tutor at the University of Wales Trinity St. David, for helping me to learn how to write better poems.
I thank you, dear reader, for taking the time to hear my voice in your ear.